10~ CREEPY CA~ JOKES

Stella Partheniou Grasso

illustrations by
Bill Dickson

Scholastic Canada Ltd.
Toronto New York London Auckland Sydney
Mexico City New Delhi Hong Kong Buenos Aires

For Nico and Sophia. Thanks for laughing at my jokes.
And for Ross, even though you didn't.
— SPG

Scholastic Canada Ltd.
604 King Street West, Toronto, Ontario M5V 1E1, Canada

Scholastic Inc.
557 Broadway, New York, NY 10012, USA

Scholastic Australia Pty Limited
PO Box 579, Gosford, NSW 2250, Australia

Scholastic New Zealand Limited
Private Bag 94407, Botany, Manukau 2163, New Zealand

Scholastic Children's Books
Euston House, 24 Eversholt Street, London NW1 1DB, UK

Library and Archives Canada Cataloguing in Publication
Partheniou Grasso, Stella
101 creepy Canadian jokes / Stella Partheniou Grasso ;
Bill Dickson, illustrator.

ISBN 978-1-4431-0771-6

1. Supernatural--Juvenile humor. 2. Monsters--Juvenile humor. 3.
Canadian wit and humor (English)--Juvenile literature.
I. Dickson, Bill II. Title.

PN6231.S877P37 2011   jC818'.602   C2011-901358-4

6 5 4 3 2 1   Printed in Canada 116   11 12 13 14 15

FROM SEA TO CREEPY SEA

What is the scariest place in Canada?

The Yukon Terrortory.

Why?

Because Yukon't *hide from the abominable snowman.*

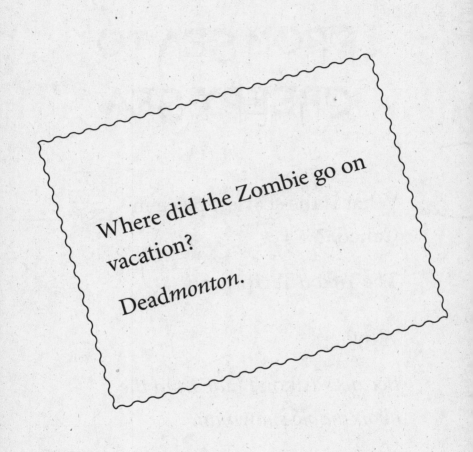

Where did the Zombie go on vacation?

Deadmonton.

Where does Bigfoot go on vacation?

Onscario.

What is the wimpiest landmark in Canada?

The CN Cower.

Why do skeletons avoid the corner of Portage and Main?

Because the wind goes right through them.

What's the scariest astronomical phenomenon?

The Northern Frights.

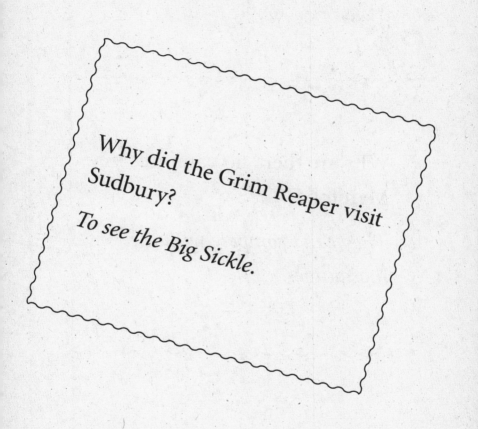

Why did the Grim Reaper visit Sudbury?

To see the Big Sickle.

Why are there no vampires in Manitoba?

They can't compete with the mosquitoes.

What do zombies farm in PEI?

Fingerling potatoes.

Why did the wraith hide in the fog off the coast of St. John's?

It wanted to be mist.

Why did the ghost go to the Calgary Stampede?

To see the nightmares.

Where did Ogopogo go on vacation?

Lake Eerie.

Why wasn't the ogre allowed on the Confederation Bridge?

He refused to pay the troll fees.

Where does Bigfoot live?

Sasquatch*ewan.*

Why did the zombie go to
Canada's Wonderland?

Because it has great roller ghosters.

Trick
or
Treat!

Trick or treat!
Who's there?
Ivana.
Ivana who?
Ivana candy, please.

Trick or treat!
Who's there?
Slime.
Slime who?
Slime freezing out here.
Let me in!

16

Trick or treat!
Who's there?
Bat.
Bat who?
Batter give me my treat before
I give you my trick.

Trick or treat!

Who's there?

Ooze.

Ooze who?

Ooze in there and why are you
hoarding all the candy?

Trick or treat!
Who's there?
Owl.
Owl who?
Owl stop knocking if you stop
hooting.

Trick or treat!

Who's there?

Witch.

Witch who?

Witching I had a treat right now.

Trick or treat!

Who's there?

Fright.

Fright who?

Fright now I'd do anything for
a candy.

Trick or treat!

Who's there?

Boo.

Boo who?

Why are you crying? I'm the one the ghost is after.

Bone Appétit!

How do ghosts take their coffee?

Double-double: two boogers, two screams.

Why was the ogress having nightmares?

It might have been someone she ate.

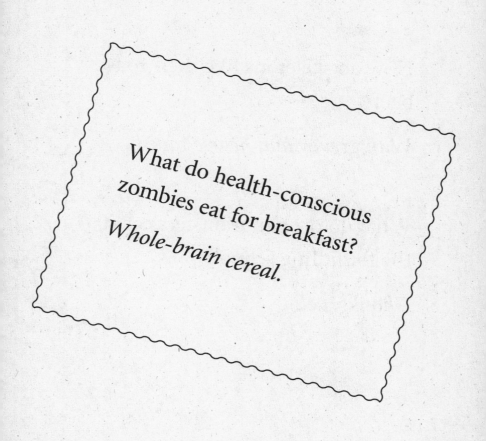

What do health-conscious zombies eat for breakfast?

Whole-brain cereal.

How do skeletons like their roast beef?

With gravey *and hearse radish.*

What do orphan monsters eat at the foundling school?

Ghoul gruel.

Where do zombie farmers store their crops?

In brain elevators.

Why did the zombie put his lunch in the ice box?

He wanted a brain freeze.

What do zombies order at the ice cream shop?

Hand shakes.

What's a banshee's favourite drink?

Scream soda.

What's a ghost's favourite food?

Ghoul*ash*.

What did the swamp monsters
serve the wizard for dinner?

Wormicelli in presto sauce.

What does a ghost eat for
breakfast?

*Scream of wheat with fresh
booberries.*

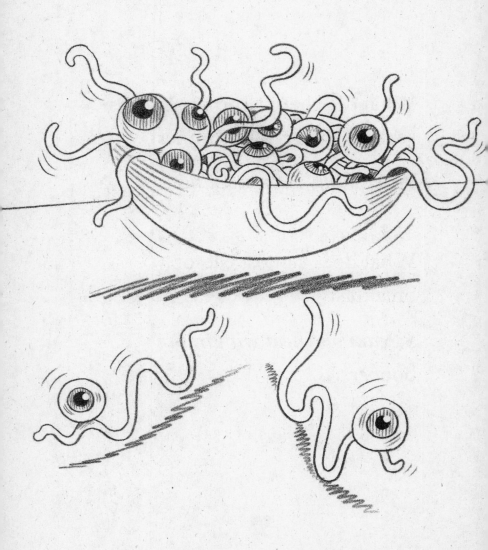

What do ghosts have for dinner?

Spookghetti and eyeballs.

BONE CUTTERS

What do you get when you cross a vampire with a snowman?

Frost bite!

How do ghosts travel in the winter?

By Ski-Boos.

Why did the abominable snowman attack the glacier?

Because it wanted to make ice scream.

Why do ghouls gather on the winter solstice?

To celebrate the longest fright of the year.

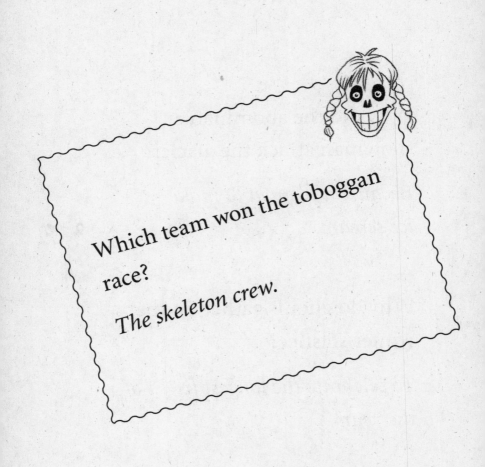

Which team won the toboggan race?

The skeleton crew.

Who's the king of the skeletons'
Winter Carnival?

Bone Homme.

CREEPY CANADA

Why do ghosts like dimes and quarters?

One has the Boonose schooner, the other has a cariboo.

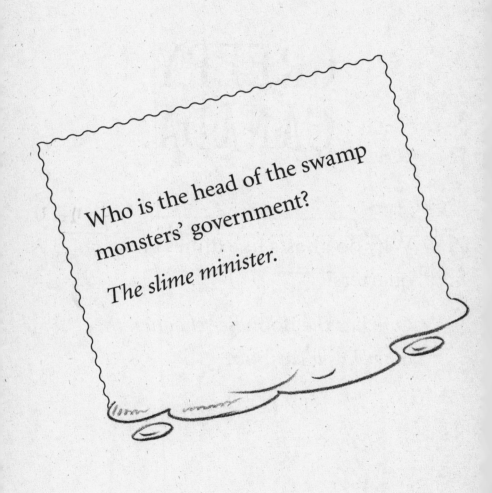

Who is the head of the swamp monsters' government?

The slime minister.

What's the capital of Creepy Canada?

Rot*tawa*.

Why did the swamp monster win the election?

Voters wanted a green candidate.

How can a poltergeist serve his country?

He can join the Ghost Guard.

How did the werewolf become Prime Minister?

He clawed his way to the top.

Why will the abominable snowman never try to eat the Peace Tower again?

It was too time-consuming.

Why did the chicken cross the road?

Because the zombie was chasing it.

Why did the *Albertosaurus* cross the road?

To escape from the terrordactyl.

Why didn't the ghost hunter cross the road?

Because he wasn't a chicken.

Why were vampires the worst prospectors?

Because they wooden stake a claim.

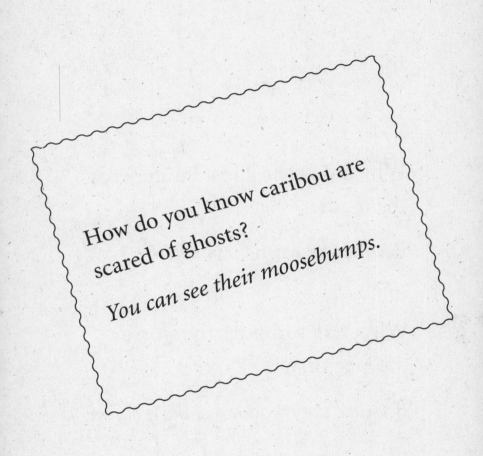

How do you know caribou are scared of ghosts?

You can see their moosebumps.

What airline do ghouls fly with?

Scare Canada.

What do you get when you cross
a vampire with a beaver?

I don't know, but I bet it has an
awful bite.

What do skeletons take with them on a camping trip?

A creepy teepee.

PARTS
AND
RE-CREATION

What's a ghost's favourite show?

Hockey Fright in Canada with Don Scary.

Where do monsters go swimming?

At the wreck centre.

What was the poltergeist's
favourite track and field event?

Shock put.

What is Frankenstein's favourite track and field event?

The 100m smash.

Why are werewolves unpopular referees?

Because they're always calling howls.

Who is the most important player on the ghosts' hockey team?

The ghoulie.

Who's the top scorer on the werewolves' hockey team?

Sidney Clawsby

What did Frankenstein do when the official fired the starter pistol?

He bolted.

Which creeps won the monsters' Brier?

The witches; no one is better with brooms.

What's a favourite winter sport
at the graveyard?

The skeleton race.

Why did the banshee join the
volleyball team?

She was a scream player.

What is a witch's favourite sport?

Cackle football.

How do vampires clean the rink?

With a Zombonie.

TOO GHOUL FOR SCHOOL

Where did the mad scientist get his degree?

*At boo*niversity.

What do banshees learn in language class?

The parts of screech.

Why did the monster raise her hand in class?

She had to go to the little ghoul's room.

Where do teenage werewolves hang out?

At the shopping maul.

What's the most popular Internet search engine?

Ghoul*gle*.

Why do wraiths make good cheerleaders?

Because they're all spirit.

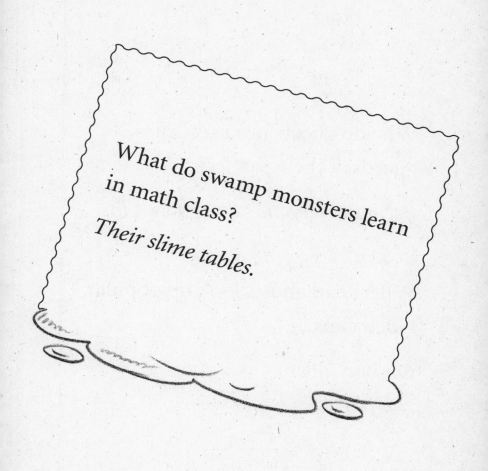

What do swamp monsters learn in math class?

Their slime tables.

Why do ghosts need security guards at their parties?

Because everyone's dying to get in.

Where can ghosts look up popular video clips?

On BooTube.

What happened when the zombie broke up with his girlfriend?

He gave her the cold shoulder.

What did the zombie give his sweetheart?

A bouquet of noses.

DR. FRANKENSTEIN, DR. FRANKENSTEIN!

Patient: Doctor, I'm having trouble sleeping.

Dr. Frankenstein: I can tell. You look dead tired.

Patient: Doctor, I'm falling to pieces.

Dr. Frankenstein: Don't worry. I'll have you stitched up in no time.

Patient: Doctor, I think I'm a skeleton.

Dr. Frankenstein: Don't be such a bonehead.

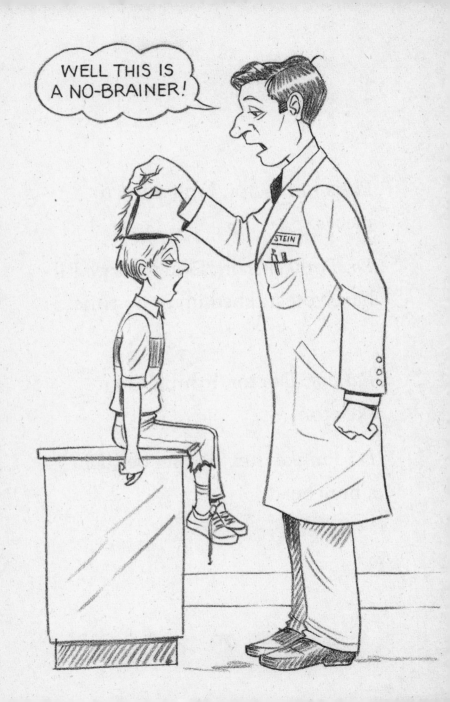

Patient: Doctor, I think I'm a zombie.

Dr. Frankenstein: Well this is a no-brainer.

Patient: Doctor, I'm having trouble smelling.

Dr. Frankenstein: That's utter nonscents.

Patient: Doctor, I think I'm a vampire.

Dr. Fankenstein: You're just a little batty, is all.

Patient: Doctor, my nightmares are out of control.

Dr. Frankenstein: Hold your horses.

Laugh Your Head Off

Why was Dr. Frankenstein such a great comedian?

Because he always left the audience in stitches.

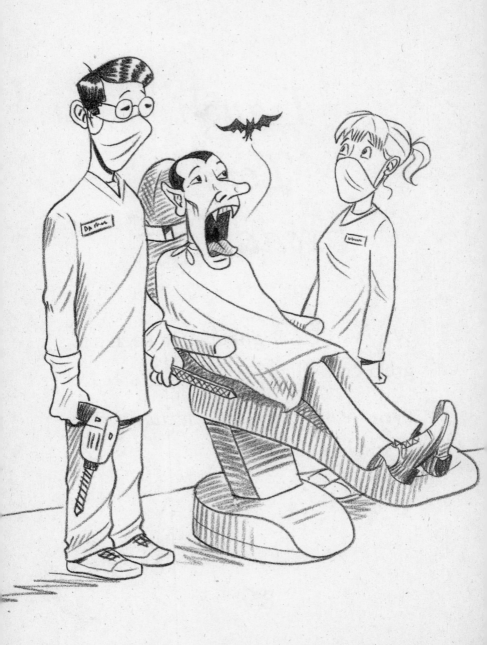

Why did the vampire go to the dentist?

To improve his bite.

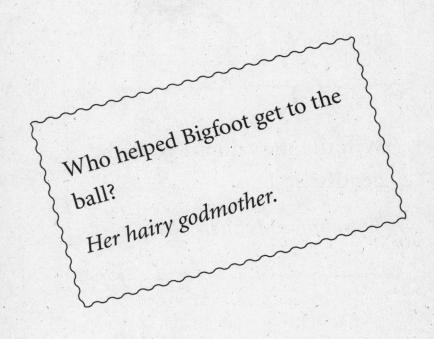

Who helped Bigfoot get to the ball?

Her hairy godmother.

Why is the invisible man such a bad liar?

Because everyone can see right through him.

What is a siren's favourite
jewellery?

Fearings.

What's a vampire's favourite
holiday?

Fangs*giving.*

What's red and white with a wicked bite?

Santa Jaws.

How did vampires come to
Canada?

On blood vessels.

Why do vampires make good
proofreaders?

*Because they can always spot the
Type Os.*

Why did the ghost get a ticket?

For haunting without a licence.

Why doesn't a ghost scream when it stubs its toe?

Because big ghouls don't cry.

Why did the witch love staying at the hotel?

Because of the great broom service.

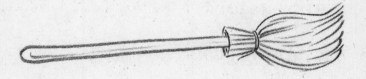